I0513415

This coloring book Belongs To:

____

copyright 2020AmirBooks
FRAIDJI AHCENE

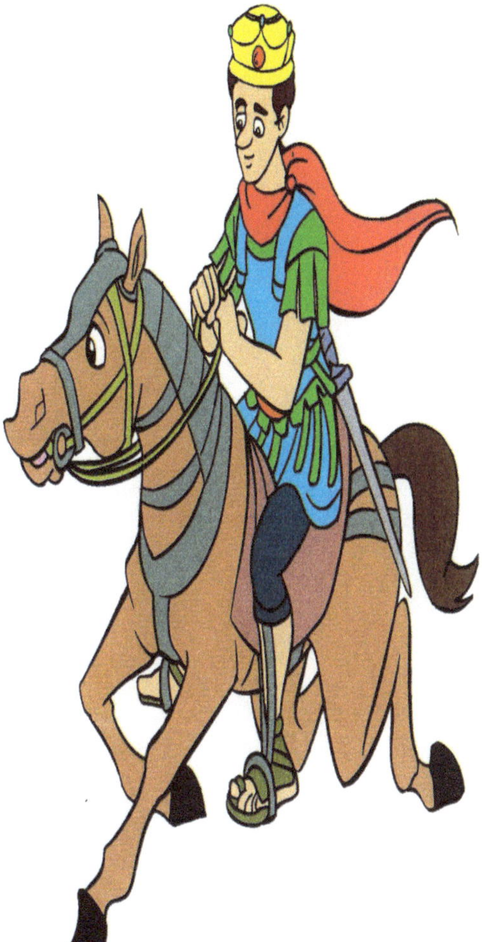

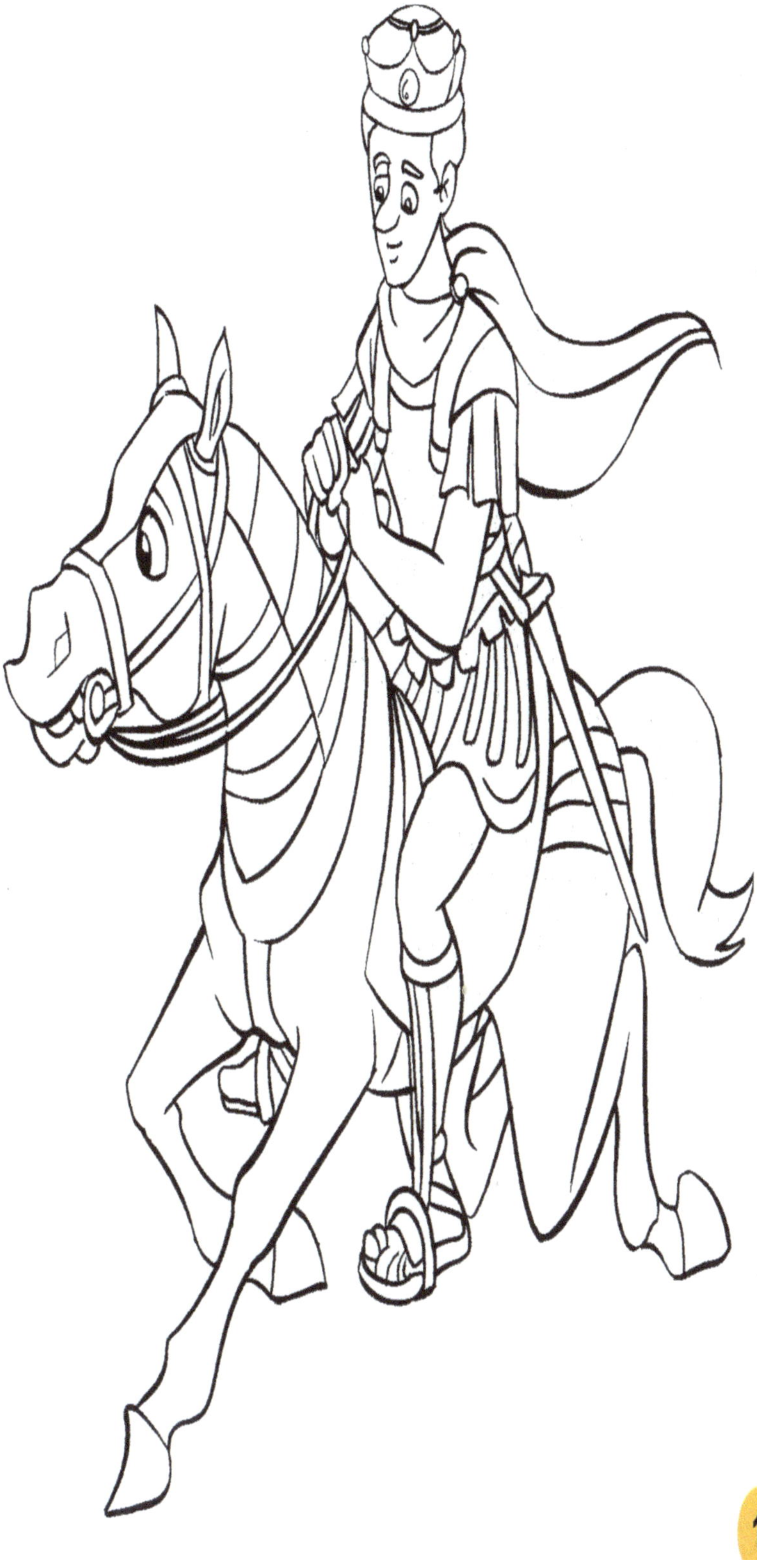

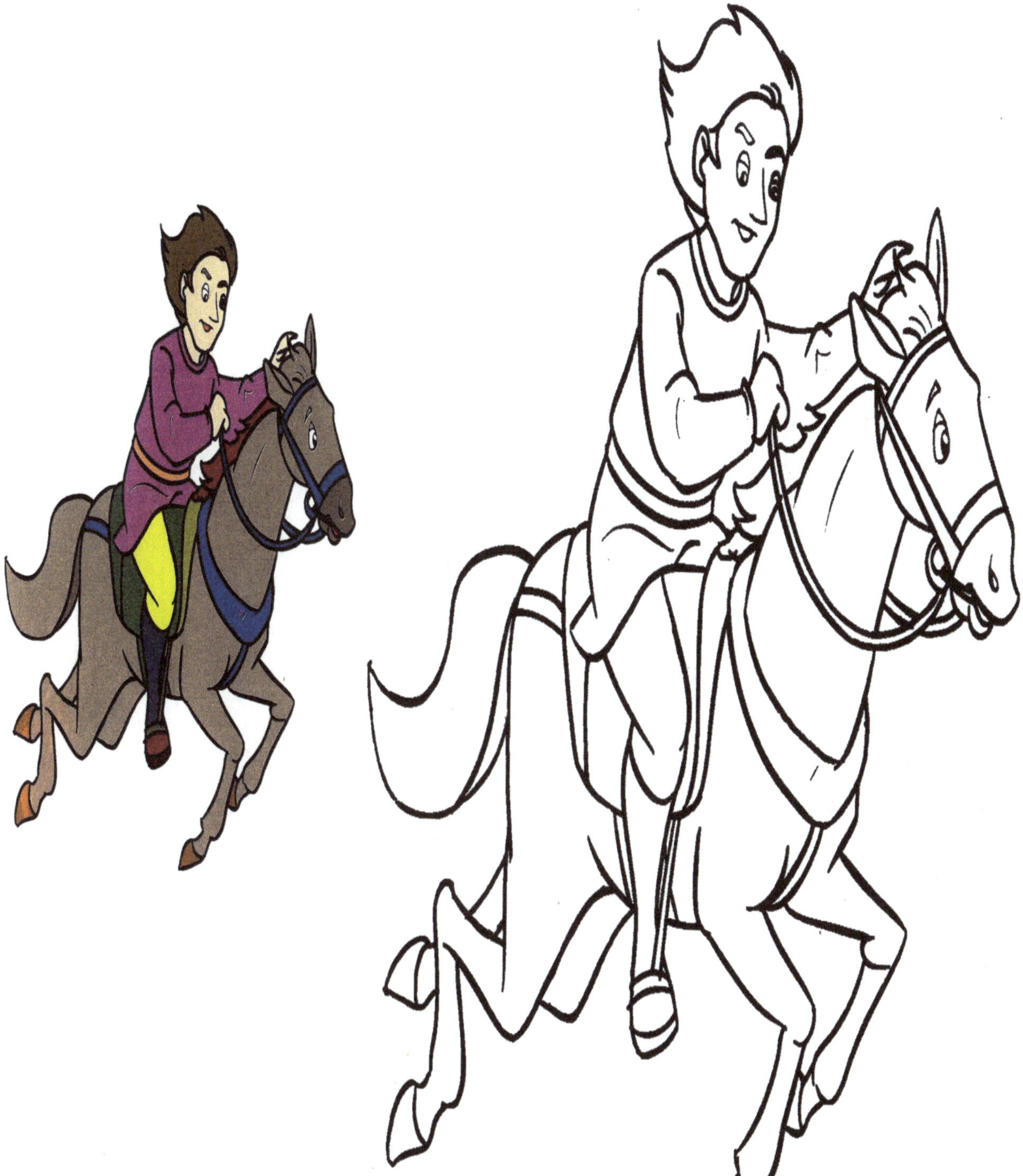

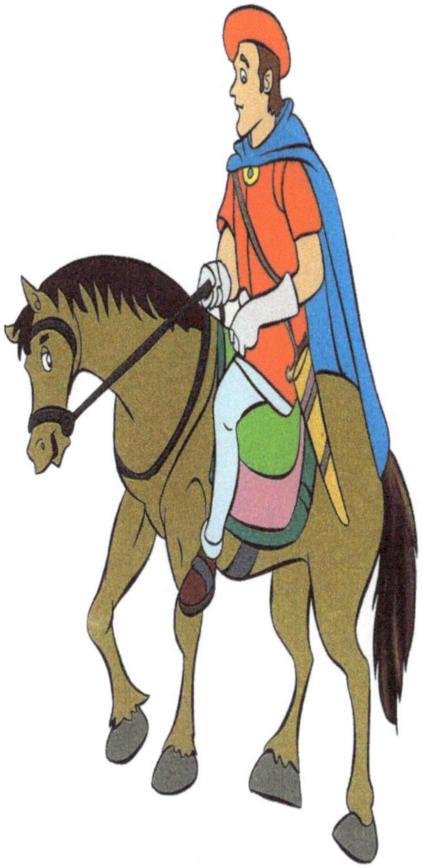

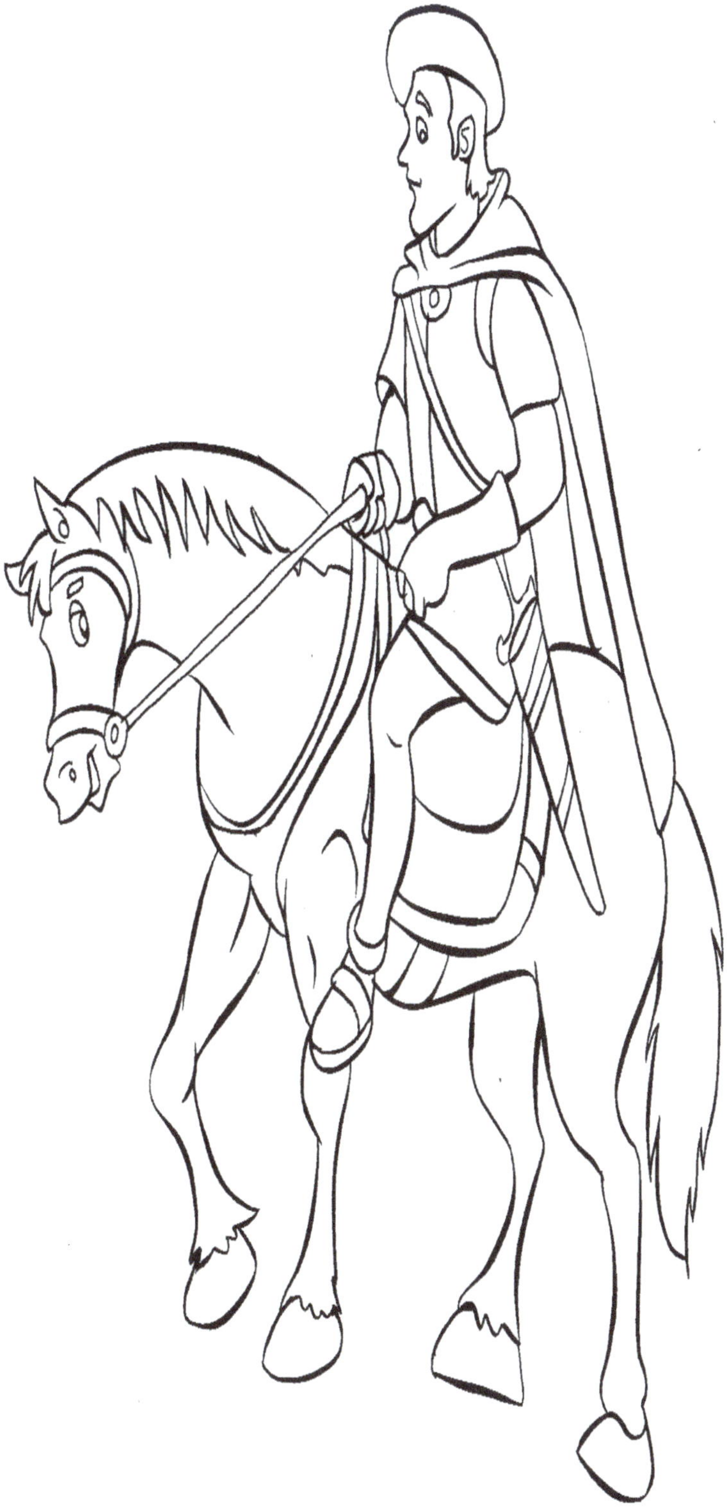

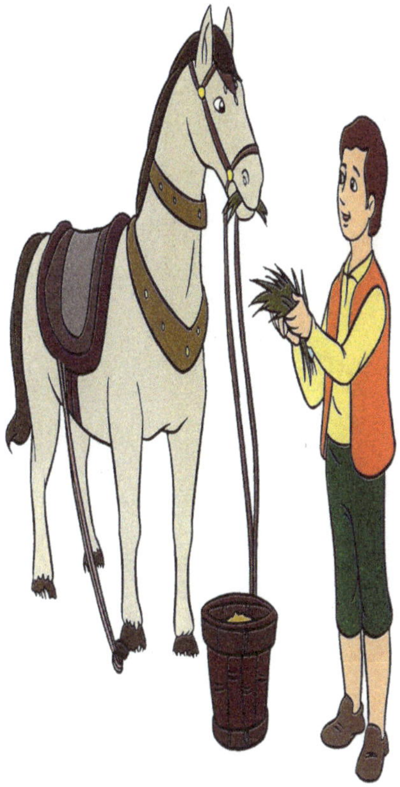

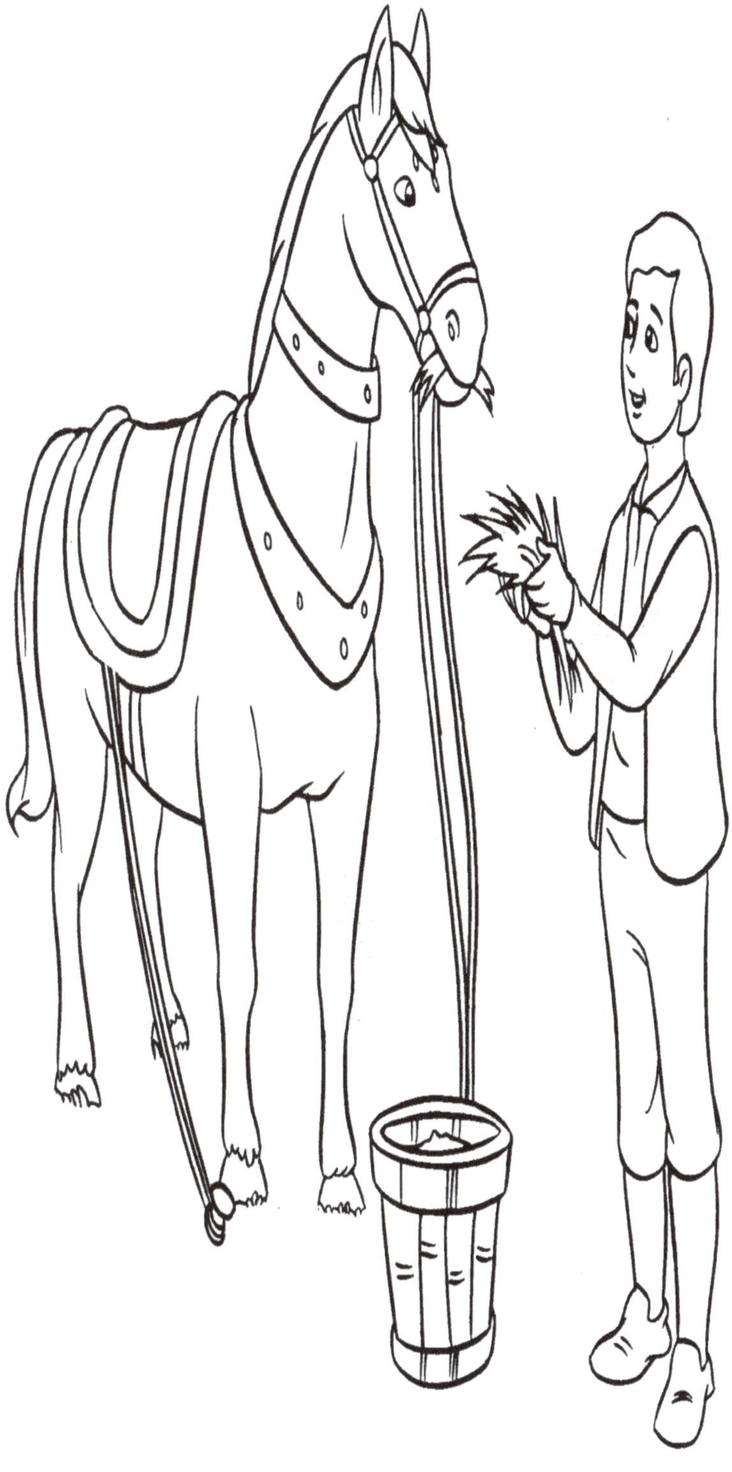

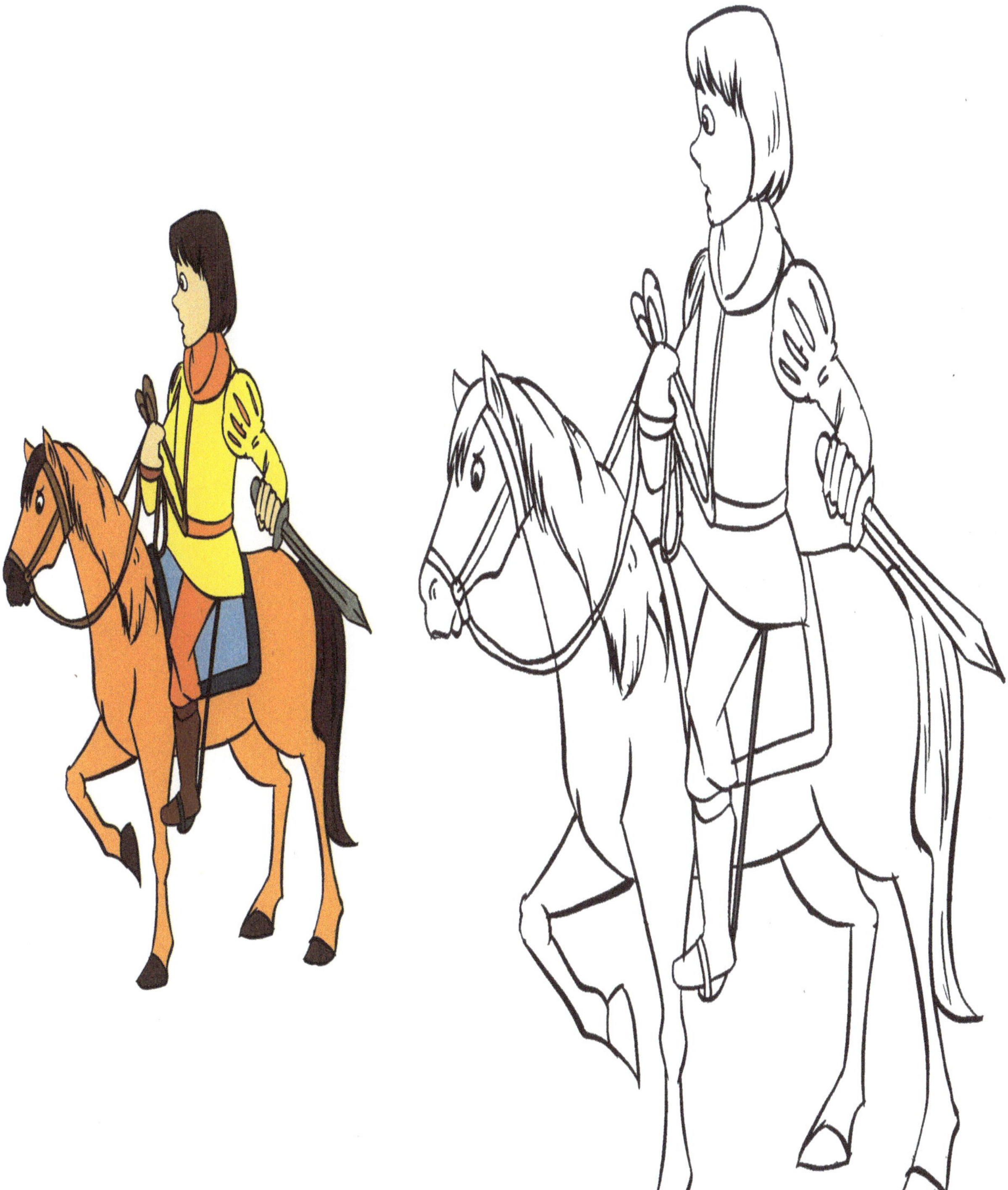

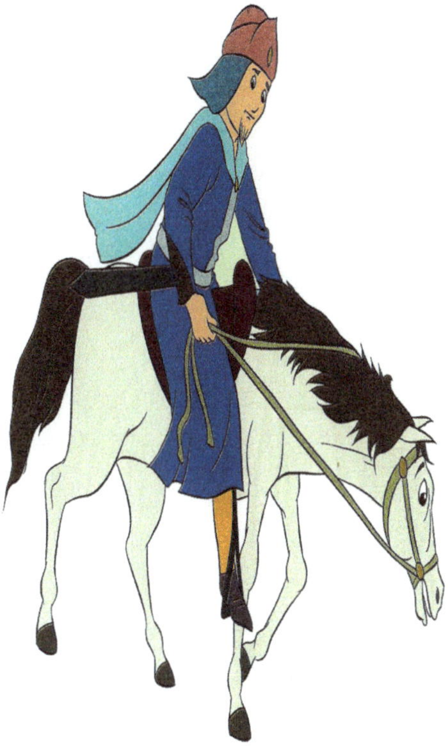

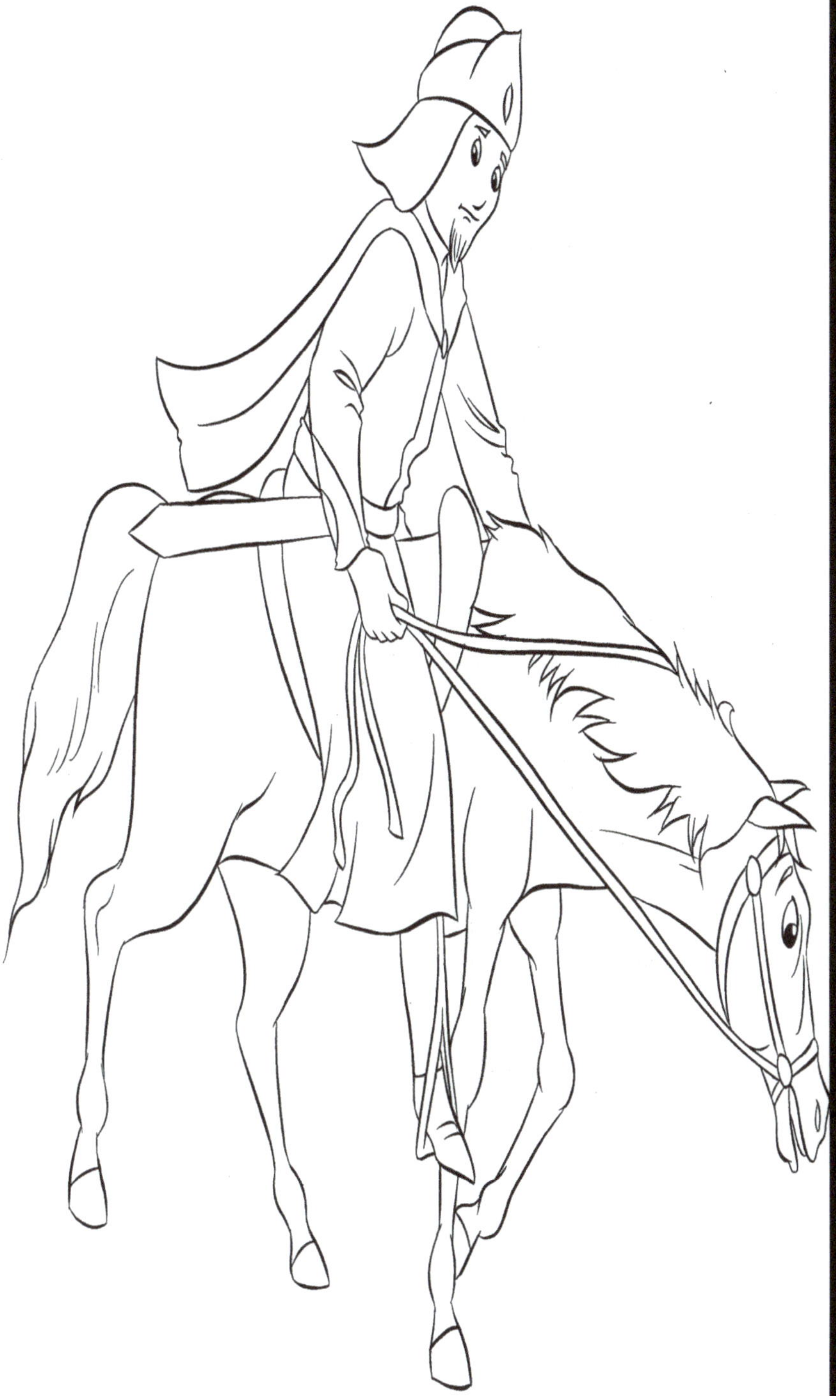

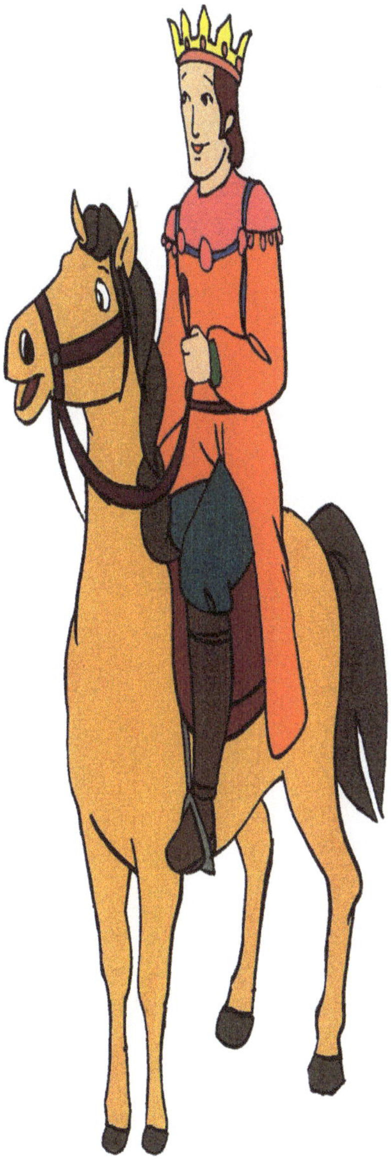
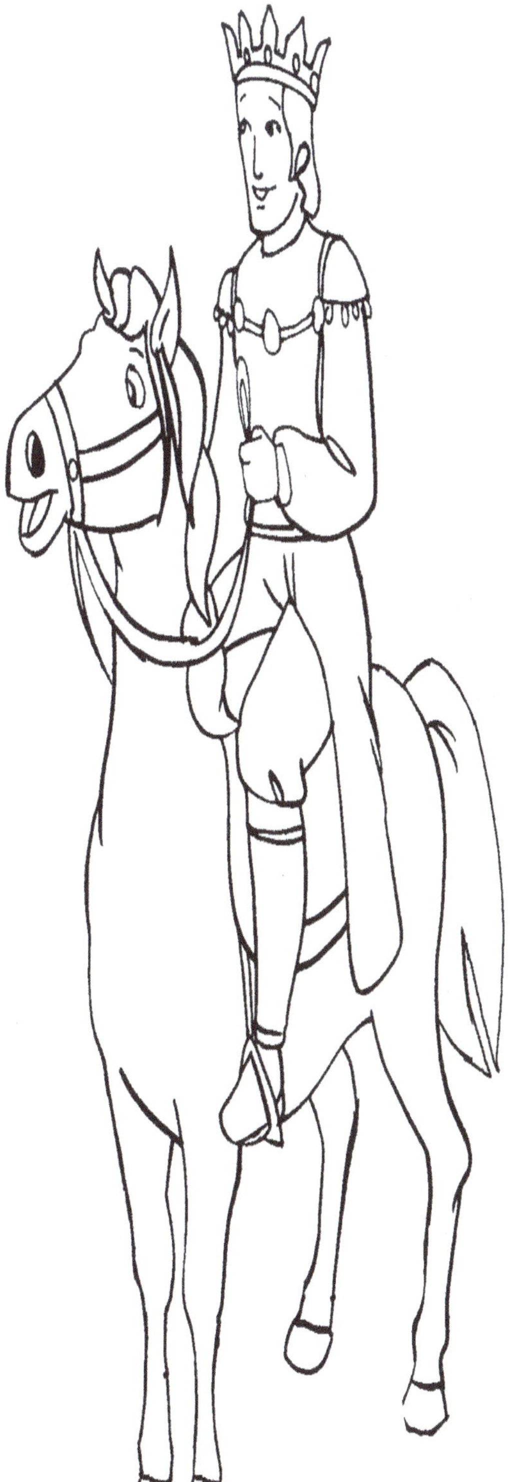

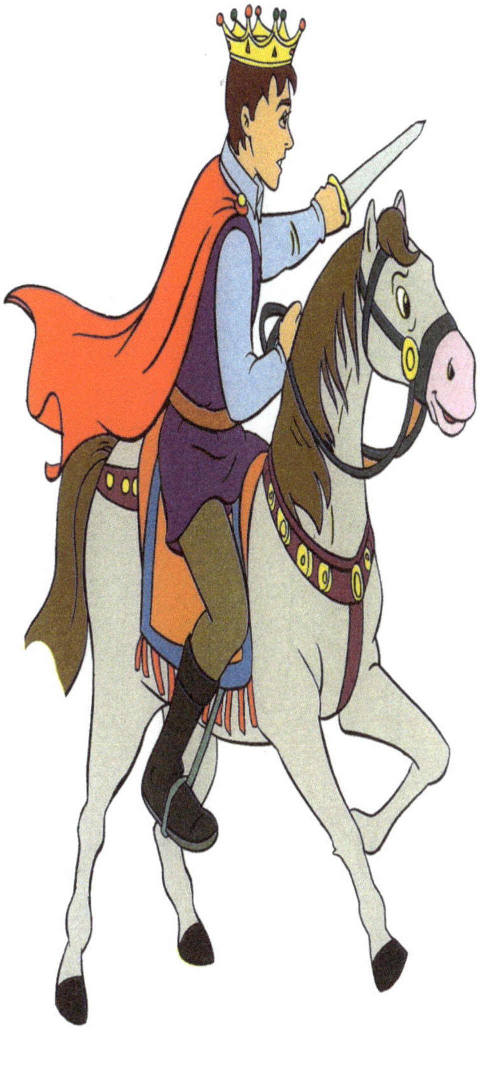

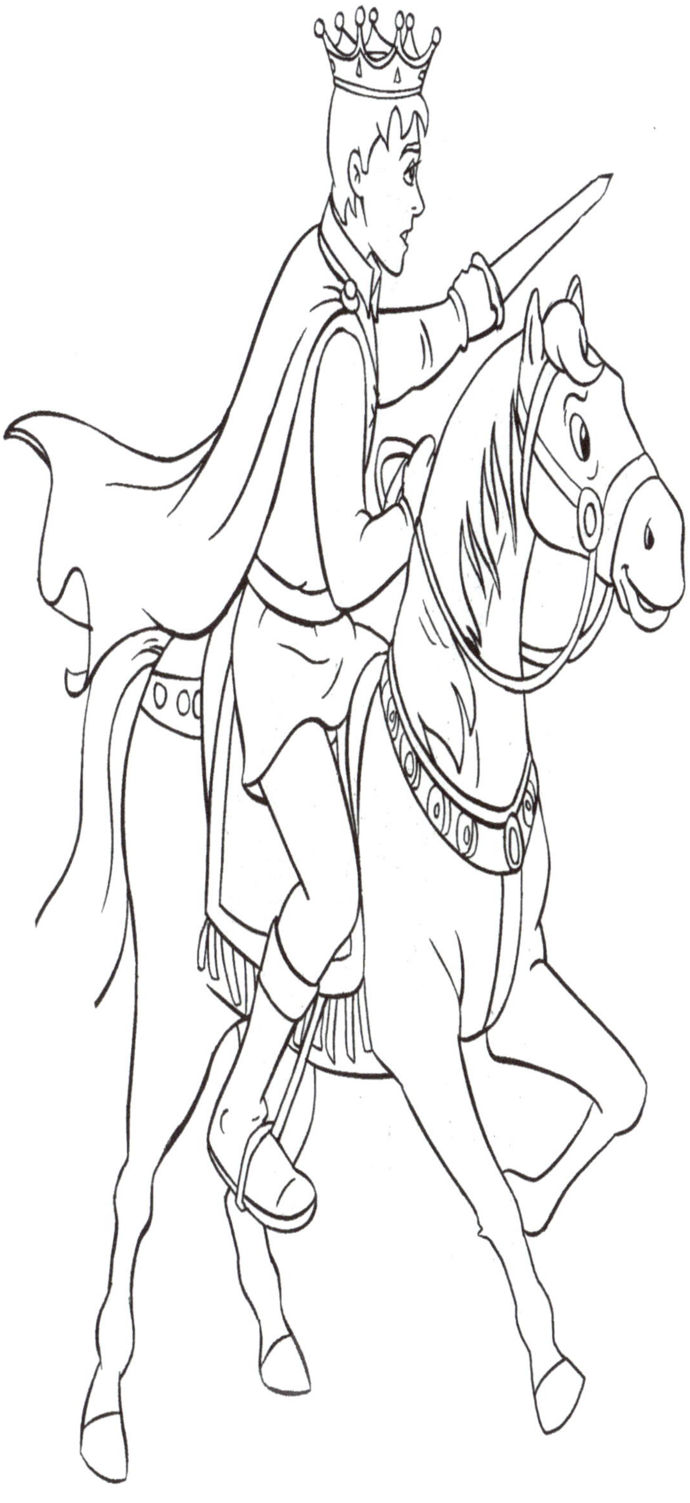

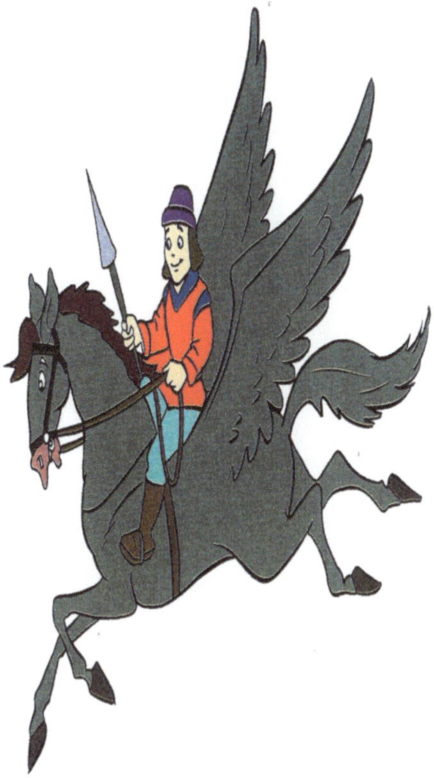

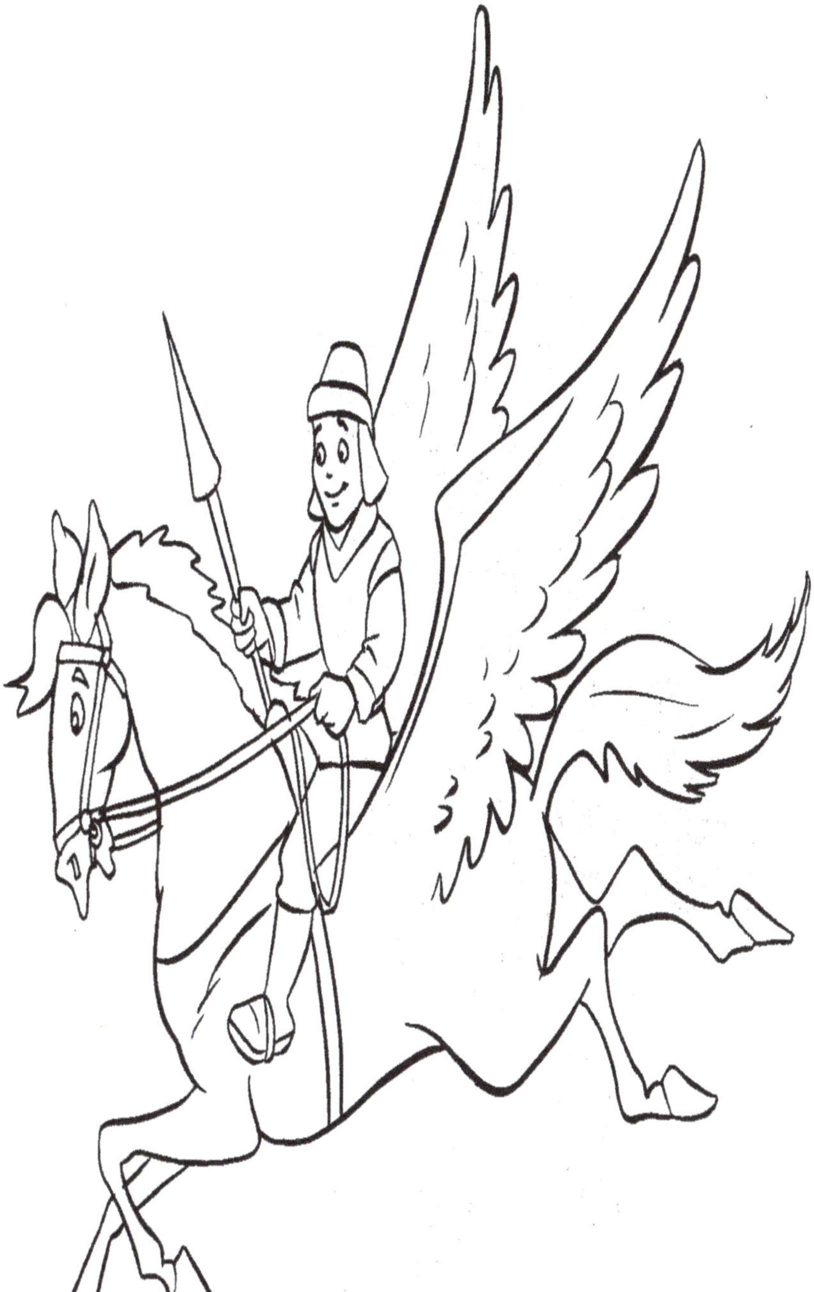

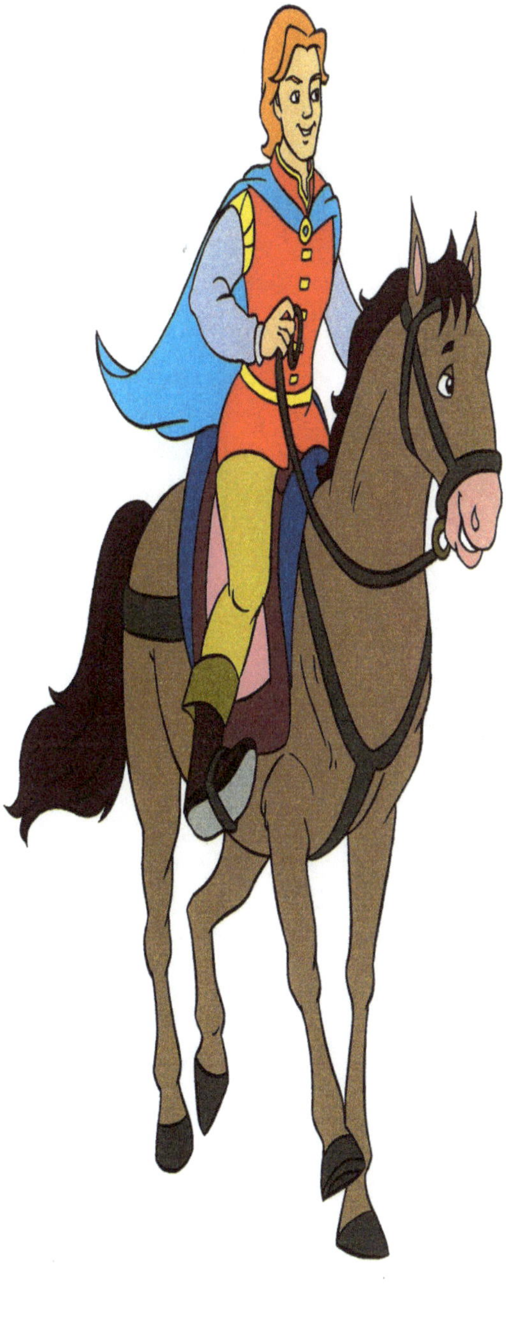

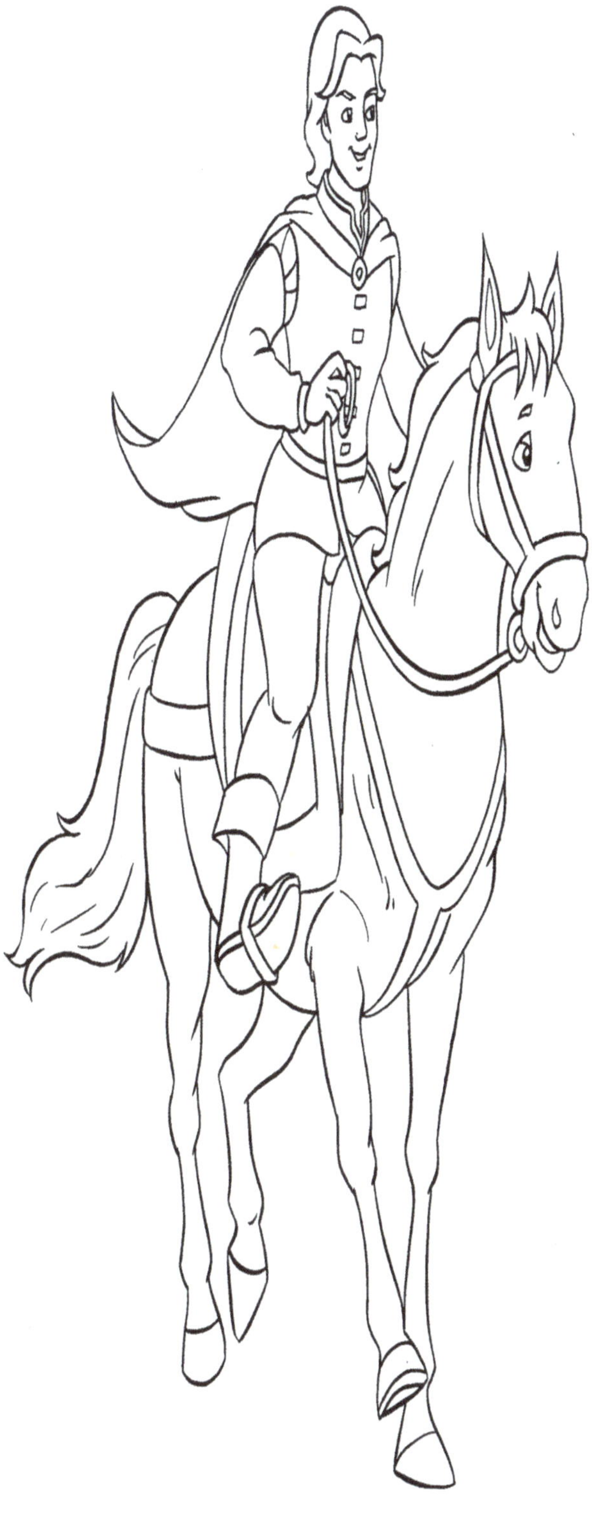

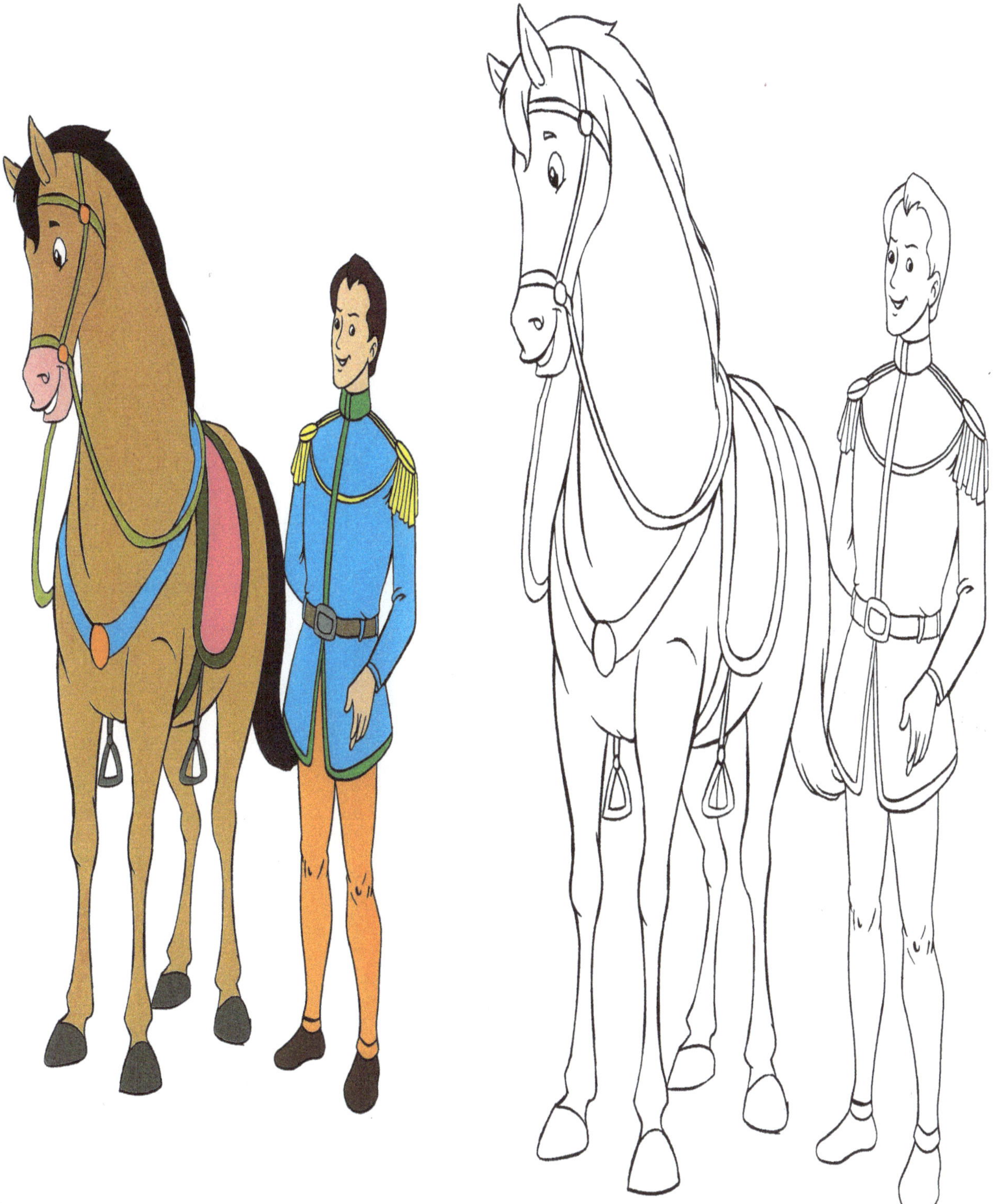

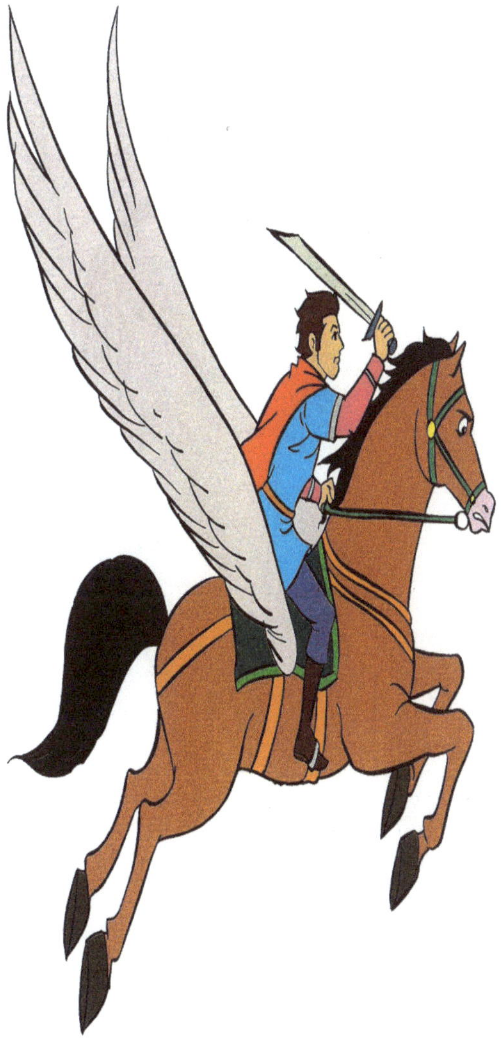

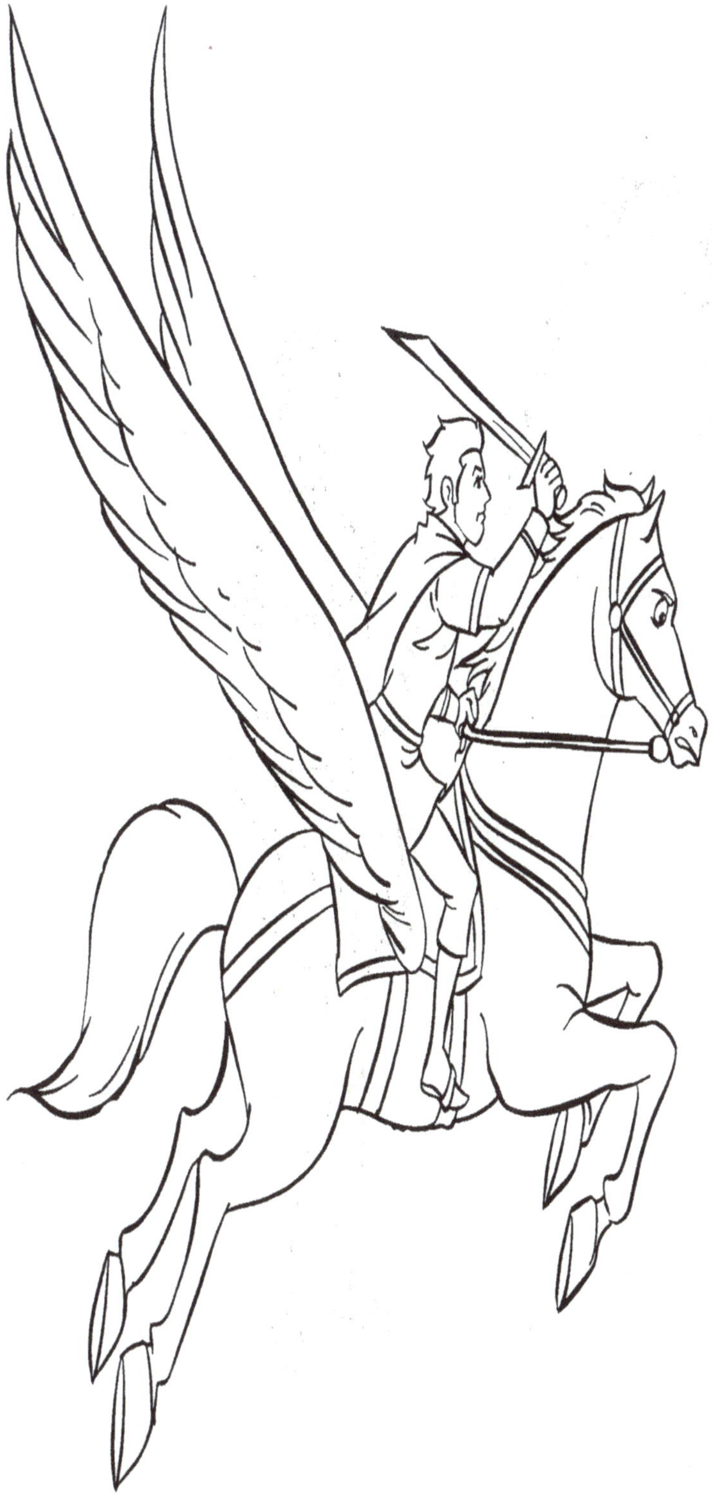

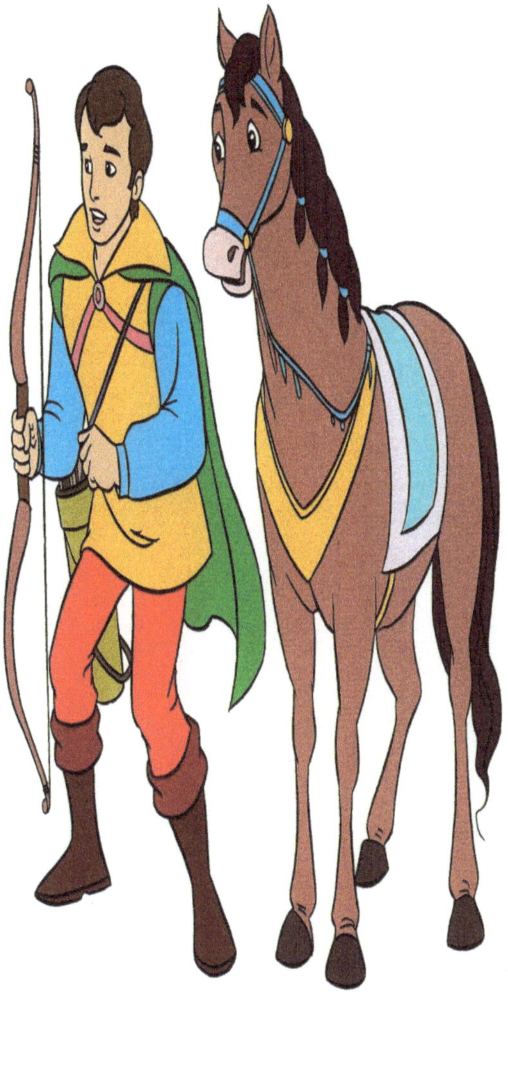

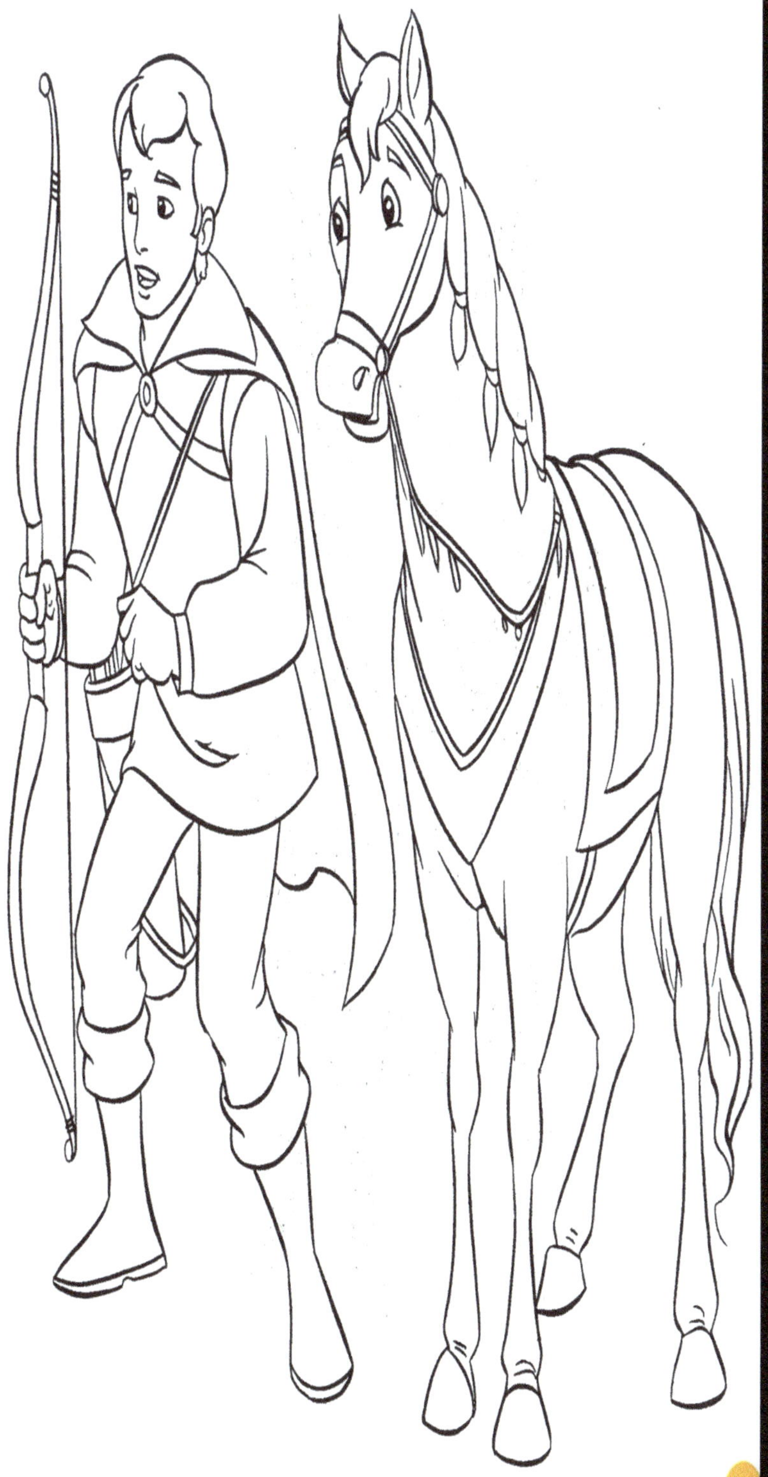

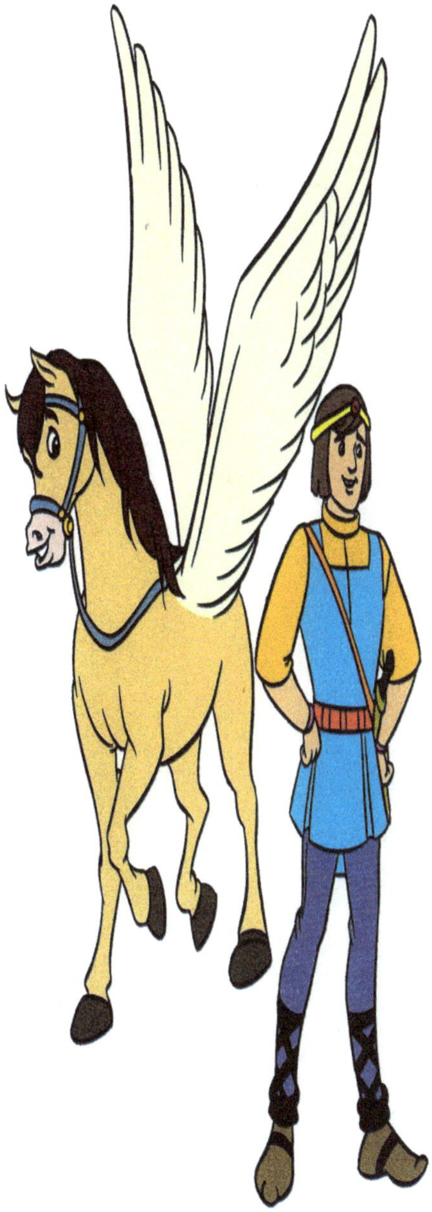

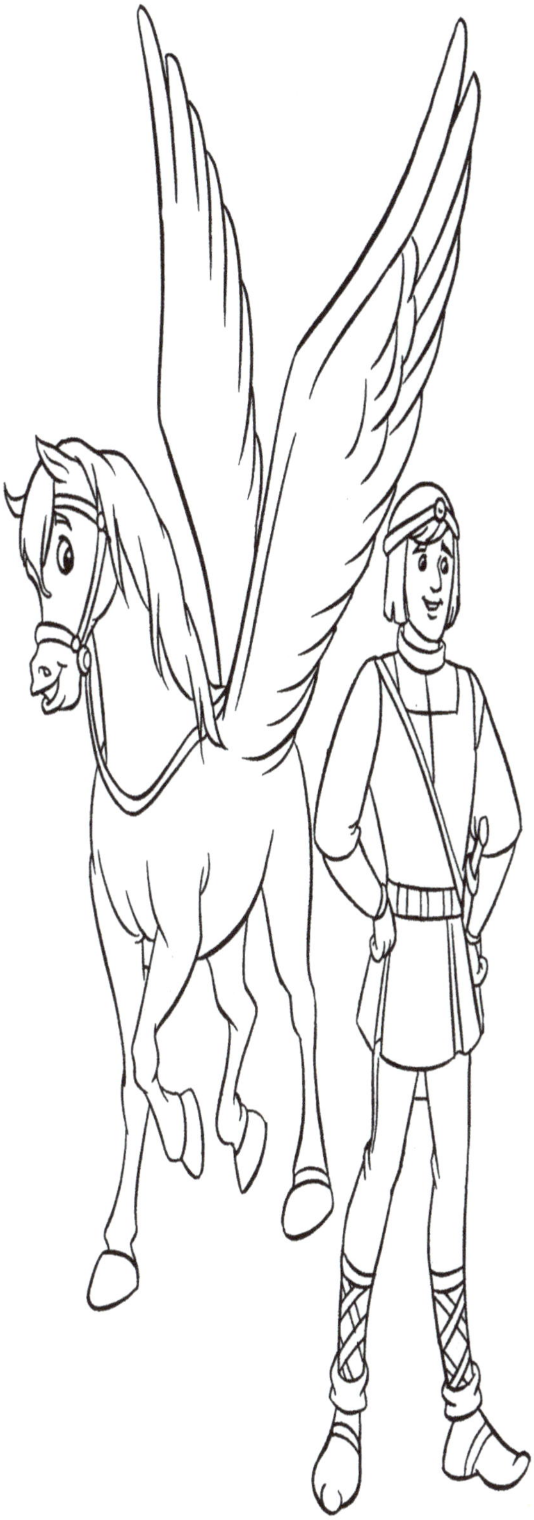

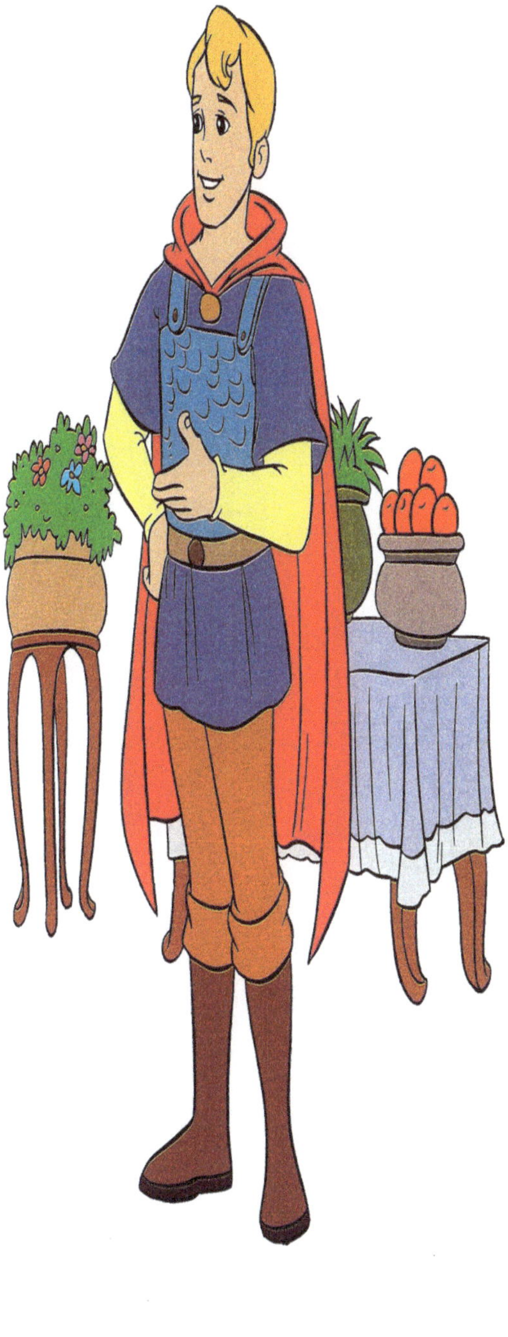

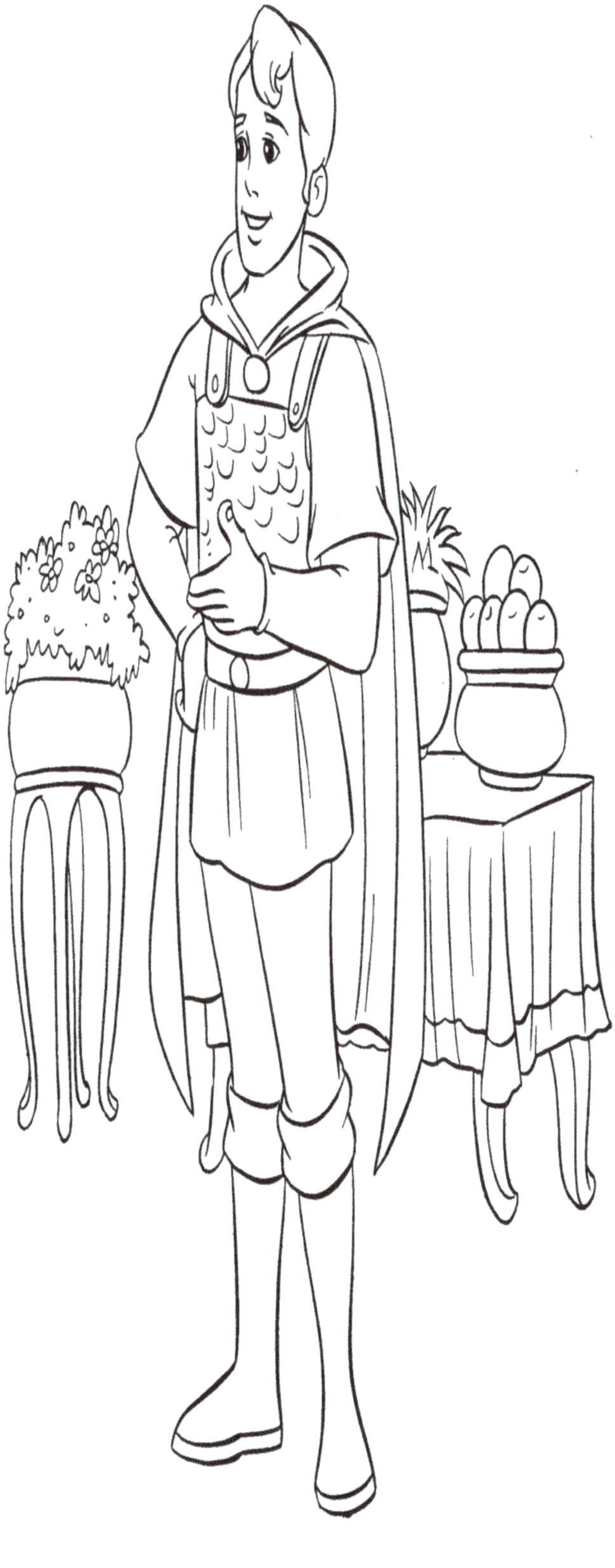

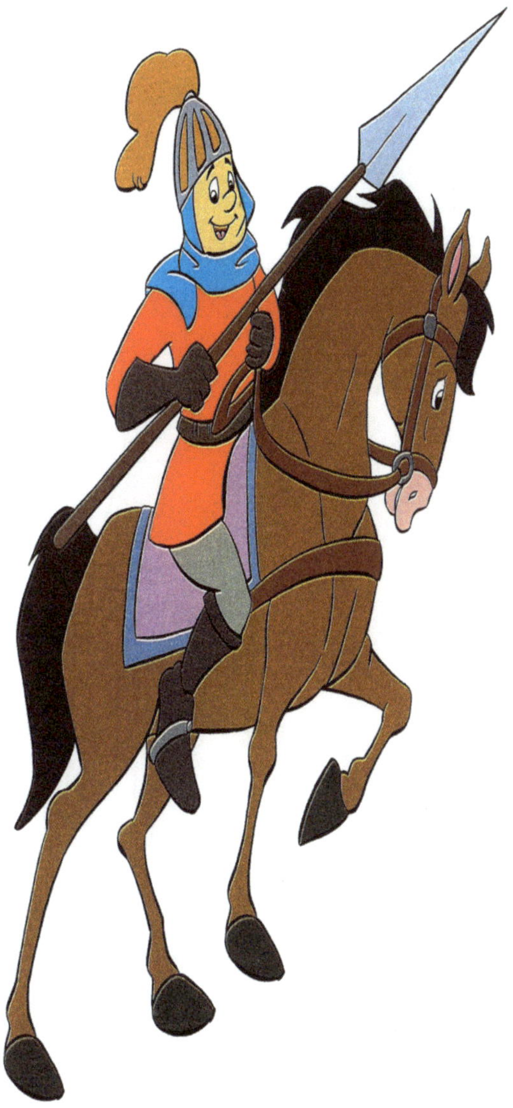

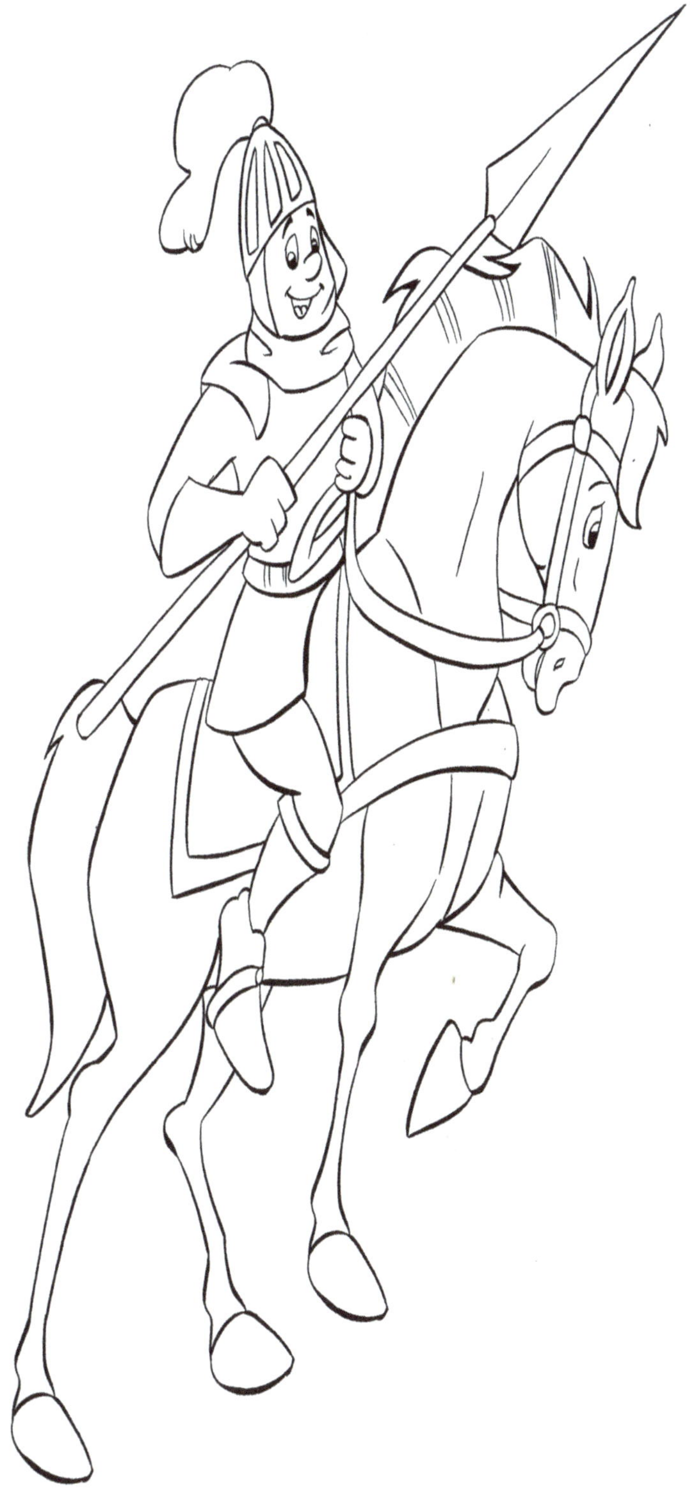

www.ingramcontent.com/pod-product-compliance
Lightning Source LLC
Chambersburg PA
CBHW041935240526
45473CB00034B/1709